Co

Preface

In researching my family's links with the medical profession over the last eight generations, it has become apparent that there is much more to it than just 400 years of medicine linked with a village in Northumberland. That in itself is remarkable enough, but I have learned a great deal about the social and diverse ways that families lived, prospered or failed over the centuries. During this time certain traits and talents beyond medicine have come to light. One such is in the life of George Fenwick of Brinkburn.

Acknowledgements

My thanks to all who have assisted me in compiling this booklet, most especially Mrs Elaine Staplins and the local historians of Old Saybrook, Connecticut who entertained us most generously when we visited. They have a fund of knowledge concerning George Fenwick's time there and about the early colonising days on the New England frontier in the seventeenth century. I have had help from Major General Euan Loudon, who kindly gave me entree to Edinburgh Castle; Canon Alan Hughes, vicar of Berwick upon Tweed, and the artist, Peter Langley. On the practical side I would like to thank Ray Huntly, Jo Lloyd and my wife Virginia for all they have done.

COLONEL GEORGE FENWICK

1603 – 1656

"A Good Man is a Public Good"

Introduction

In the year 2000, General Sir Michael Rose, Colonel of the Coldstream Guards, laid up the regimental colours of the 2nd Battalion above Colonel George Fenwick's memorial in Berwick Parish Church, by kind permission of Her Majesty Queen Elizabeth II. The Service, led by the vicar of Berwick, Canon Alan Hughes, also of the Coldstream Guards, commemorated the three hundred and fiftieth anniversary of the formation of the regiment at the Battle of Dunbar in 1650, and in the same year the building of Berwick Parish Church. Significantly, it honoured the contribution that Colonel George Fenwick had given to both.

General Rose's act not only signified the important links that exist between the Coldstream Guards, the town of Berwick-upon-Tweed and Colonel George Fenwick but also celebrated the remarkable life of "a Good Man". George Fenwick's life was full and varied, spanning colonies and continents. He exhibited gallantry and religious tolerance during a precarious period of English history. Huge changes took place with the pendulum of power swinging from absolute Monarch to Commonwealth, then back to a Constitutional Monarch. George was involved in all that was happening and had gifts and qualities that set him above many, making him a uniquely popular man of his time.

Chapter I

Brinkburn Priory and the Early Fenwicks

George Fenwick's family lived at Brinkburn Priory on the Coquet River in the centre of the county of Northumberland, approximately 40 miles south of Berwick. A branch of the Fenwick family originally settled here in 1546, shortly after its Dissolution.

The Priory, in the parish of Longframlington was founded in about 1135 by William Bertram of Mitford. It was the branch of a Priory near Pentney in Norfolk called St Mary de Insula.

The Priory took about forty years to build. The master builder was a man called Roger Colutarius who built a number of churches in Northumberlandand. Brinkburn is in a secluded area of the Coquet valley on a bend in the river with tall cliffs to the south and a wooded hillside to the north and had twelve Augustinian Canons in residence.

The style of architecture lies between Norman and Early English. The arches of the arcades and most of the lower tiers of the lancet windows have the pointed heads of Early English architecture, but all the main doors and upper windows, although obviously built later, are in the rounded Norman or Romanesque style. The visitor's first view as he descends the track to the river is the magnificent round-arched northern door with extensive stone ornamentation, framed by the trees that surround it. Above this can be seen the Early English arcade of three trefoiled and pointed arches on detached shafts.

Brinkburn North Door   *Painting by Peter Langley*

Although the Priory is only 40 metres long the proportions are designed to give it a feeling of being much bigger. The Priory is described in The County History of Northumberland as being "a spare and dignified building, beautifully proportioned and ornamented with delicate detail."

At the time of the Dissolution of the Monasteries when the priory was laid waste much of the ornamentation was removed. There is one small statue still to be seen on the eastern side of the church where the chancel roof meets the wall of the tower.

The monks would have grown medicinal plants and herbs in the Priory garden for themselves and the people of the locality. In certain Monasteries monks had hospitals and cared for the sick within their Monastery, but Brinkburn was too small to sustain this. In spite of its secluded position it was raided regularly by marauding Scots, who reduced it to poverty with monotonous regularity. From time to time letters were sent complaining about the poverty imposed upon the monks by such frequent raids; sadly these are almost the only documents that remain concerning life at the Priory.

In 1322 the Priory petitioned the King for relief from the poverty resulting from the losses they had sustained. Over the years the monks were given help and foodstuffs by the King, but raids from Scotland continued. In 1419 they lost charters, muniments, books, chalices, vestments, ornaments and other goods.

A tale is told that on one occasion, news reached the monks that the Scots were coming but, because of their secluded position, the reivers passed by, leaving the Priory unmolested. Foolishly the monks celebrated their escape from further destruction by ringing the church bell. The Scots, who were not far away, heard the bell and so found their way to the Priory. They threw the bell into a deep pool in the Coquet where it rests to this day in what is known as the Bell Pool. It is said that on a clear day you can make out the shape of the bell, lying at the bottom of the pool.

In spite of the threat of Greater Excommunication passed on them by the Bishop of Durham in 1419 the Scots continued to raid remorselessly. As a result Brinkburn Priory was never a wealthy house. However, the monks did succeed in hiding some of their wealth, for in 1834 some workmen, who were clearing away a burnt- out wooden building situated to the northwest of the church, removed a hearthstone. The man throwing up the spoil from under the stone onto a cart commented to his mate on the cart that it was the heaviest spadeful he had ever thrown. His mate looked down and saw a pot made of brass, and in it a collection of gold coins. The coins, from the reigns of Edward III and Richard II, are now to be seen in the British Museum and are known as the Brinkburn Horde. This treasure had obviously been hidden by the monks, and who knows if there is more elsewhere? The Scots clearly thought so, as their regular incursions to Brinkburn continued unabated in spite of the dire threat from the Bishop.

The end of the Priory came in February 1536 with the visitation from Henry VIII's Commissioners, Drs Layton and Legh. They reported that the Canons venerated the girdle of St Peter as a relic, and that William Hogeson, the Prior, was alleged to be "incontinent with divers women." Under the Act of Dissolution in 1536 the house was dissolved and the prior was given a pension of £11 per year. The Priory at Brinkburn consisted of the church, demesne lands, grange, two orchards, gardens, a watermill and a tannery as well as surrounding farm land. There was no evidence of it including a hospital. The total annual income of the Priory was calculated in that year to be £94.9s.2d.

The links between Brinkburn Priory and the Fenwick family began after the Dissolution of the Priory. The land was first leased to Cuthbert Carnaby but in 1546 before that lease was ended, a new lease for forty years was granted to George Fenwick, the son of Gerard Fenwick and grandson of Sir John Fenwick of Wallington.

This lease was from John Dudley (1501–53), Earl of Warwick, who was created Duke of Northumberland soon after. He had usurped the Duke of Somerset as Protector of the young Edward VI (1537–52) and for a short time in the latter part of Edward's reign, John Dudley was the most ruthless and powerful man in England. When Edward VI died the Duke of Northumberland sponsored his own daughter-in-law, the Protestant Lady Jane Grey, to become Queen. Having persuaded Edward to leave her the throne in his Will, the Duke suffered the consequences of meddling with the Succession and was ousted from power by the other members of the Council of State. These were determined to have Edward's Catholic half-sister Mary, as Queen. Dudley therefore followed Protector Somerset to the Tower of London and thence to the execution block. His lands reverted to the Crown.

There was a great deal of power-broking going on at this turbulent time. Queen Mary in 1557 gave the lands previously held by John Dudley, Duke of Northumberland, to Thomas Percy (1528–72), who became the heir to Henry, the sixth Earl of Northumberland. Sir Thomas Percy, (Thomas's father) had been executed at Tyburn in 1537 for taking part in the Pilgrimage of Grace, a rebellion by the Catholic gentry of England in protest against Henry VIII's break with Rome and the Dissolution of the Monasteries. Thomas Percy was an ardent Catholic and follower of Queen Mary but he could not inherit the title as seventh Earl of Northumberland when Henry, the sixth Earl, died because his father, Sir Thomas, had been attainted at the time of The Pilgrimage of Grace. Thus he, Thomas lost his chance of inheriting that title and it went into abeyance. However, in 1557 Queen Mary created Thomas, Baron Percy instead and, on the following day, she made him Earl of Northumberland –- the first Earl of the second creation.

At about the same time, George Fenwick assigned his lease of Brinkburn to his younger brother Tristram, so that by the accession of Queen

Elizabeth in 1558, the land at Brinkburn was owned by Thomas, Earl of Northumberland, and leased to Tristram Fenwick.

Both men then became involved in the Rising of The North in 1569. This was another insurrection, again by the Catholic northern Earls, with the object of releasing Mary Queen of Scots from her English prison, making her Queen of England, thereby turning England back to the Catholic faith. This Rising was ruthlessly suppressed and both Thomas Percy and Tristram Fenwick were captured. Tristram had his lands at Brinkburn taken from him, while Thomas Percy, who had escaped into Scotland after the Rising, was betrayed by Hector Armstrong of Liddesdale and handed over to James Stewart, Earl of Moray, who imprisoned him in Lochleven Castle for nearly three years. After a huge bribe Percy was then given up to the Governor of Berwick, who immediately sent him to York where he was beheaded on August 22, 1572. Thus the first two owners of Brinkburn Priory after its Dissolution perished by execution. It did not bode well for future owners.

Although his leased land was taken from him, it appears that Tristram Fenwick continued to live at Brinkburn and may well have received some form of pardon. He was succeeded by his son George.

There were no direct family records at that time and these details of the family are taken from the History of Northumberland which quotes as its source of information the Heralds' visitations of 1615 and 1666. These have been labelled by Percy Hedley, the antiquarian author of 'Northumberland Families', as containing many apocryphal descents which he says abounded in the 16th and 17th centuries. He comments:

"It is generally inadvisable to accept no more than two or three generations of these visitation pedigrees without any confirmatory evidence. In most cases the head of the family just produced a pedigree which was accepted without question by the herald, When a man did not know the name of his grandmother, it seems unlikely that he had much knowledge of his grandfather. No doubt he could have got the necessary knowledge from his

family documents, but could he read?"

It is therefore important to realise that any information about a large and diverse family during this time is based on hearsay evidence. Another problem in tracing these family trees is that names were frequently the same in consecutive generations while the dates given for births and deaths were often erroneous. When dealing with a large county clan like the Fenwicks this allows a great deal of mistaken identity and variations of pedigree. The size of this clan is well described in "The Ballad of The Redeswire Raid" (which took place in 1575) as follows:

> *"I saw come marching owre the knowes*
> *Five hundred Fenwicks in a flock*
> *with jack and speir and bowes all bent*
> *and warlike weapons at their will."*

The job of the amateur genealogist is challenging and quite impossible to prove the descents described: some errors in these family trees are to be expected.

In spite of this it seems certain that George Fenwick, living at Brinkburn at the turn of the 17th century and who died in 1617, had five sons. He also had three daughters. Two of his sons died young. The eldest son, who was also called George, is the man honoured in Berwick Parish Church and the hero of this book.

FAMILY TREE OF GEORGE FENWICK OF BRINKBURN

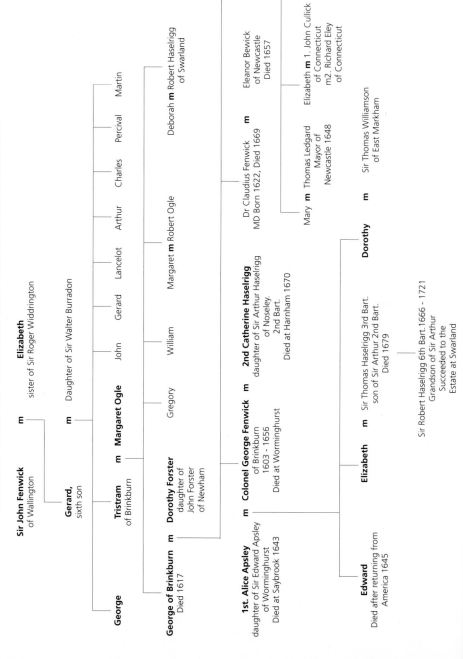

Chapter II

Early Life and Creation of the Warwick Patentees

George was born in 1603, the year of the death of Elizabeth I and the arrival of James I onto the English throne. This change of monarch had huge consequences for the Border region which for years had withstood the raids from Scotland and mounted many reiving raids from England in return. Indeed the Fenwick clan were amongst the most frequent raiders into Scotland throughout the troubled times on the Border Marches. James I had great difficulty dealing with this wild borderland. He decided that the best way to stop the constant brigandage, blood feuds and petty warfare on the Border between the two countries, now united under the same monarch, was to transport the worst offenders. He exiled whole clans to Ireland while at the same time the Duke of Buccleuch took a legion of some of the worst and most desperate of the Border warriors to fight in Holland against Spain:

"The warriors had as much reason to rejoice on their arrival upon the Continent as Britain to congratulate herself upon their departure."
(Sir Walter Scott)

Perhaps some of the violence seen in Ireland since 1603 originally began on the English and Scottish border.

George Fenwick grew up at Brinkburn with his brothers and sisters. Their parents were George Fenwick and his wife, Dorothy, daughter of John Forster of Newham. The older George had a sister called Deborah who married Robert Haselrigg of Old Swarland whose cousin was Sir Arthur Haselrigg, who soon comes into this story. The Haselrigg family had been at Swarland since the 14th century: another branch lived at Eslington. It was through the Forster family that young George was able to buy back the land at Brinkburn which his grandfather had earlier forfeited. The land had been acquired by Sir John Forster, who was the Warden of the Middle March (the central Borders on the English side) for most of Queen Elizabeth's reign and was only forced from office at the ripe old age of 94. George purchased the land back from Edward Forster, a grandson of Sir John and a cousin of his mother.

There are no details about George's early education, but it is possible that he was tutored by a cousin Sir Claudius Forster after whom George's brother Claudius was named and who lived about six miles from Brinkburn at Wreighburn in Thropton.

George's education, proved good enough for him to go to Cambridge University where he read law at Queens' College. Oliver Cromwell was at Sidney Sussex College at about the same time. There is no evidence that they knew each other then, nor when they were both called to the Bar; Cromwell to Lincolns Inn and George to Gray's Inn. However, they would have become acquainted when George became

Queens' College, Cambridge

Agent to the Warwick Patentees. He probably became Agent through nepotism as his uncle Robert Haselrigg was a cousin of Sir Arthur Haselrigg, a Patentee. These were a group of Puritan aristocrats sharing Cromwell's political allegiances and who in 1631 had been given patents by James I, later confirmed by Charles I, allowing them to colonise an area of New England. The Patentees were the Earl of Warwick, and a small number of his family and friends. Warwick was President of the Council of New England originally set up by James I.

There was growing tension between Parliamentary (largely Puritan) and Royalist (largely Catholic) factions in England. Two of the leading Puritan Lords involved in the continuing Parliamentary struggles were **Lord Saye and Sele**, of Broughton Castle, Banbury, and **Lord Brooke**, of Warwick Castle. Lord Saye and Sele was nicknamed "Old Subtlety" by Charles I as he was always scheming in the Parliamentary interest against the Royalist faction. Lord Brooke was to be killed in the Civil War in 1643 by a stray bullet when leading his regiment in the Siege of Lichfield. In 1636, however, both were among the Patentees, as was **Charle Fiennes** son of Lord Saye and Sele.

Lord Saye and Sele   *Lord Brooke*

Some claim that the town of Saybrook in Connecticut owes it's name to these Lords, but others think it was named by the Dutch who first settled there as Zeebrugge, and that the first English settlers anglicised it to link it with these two noble Patentees.

Other Patentees included: **Lord Holland; Lord Rich,** who was related to the Earl of Warwick; **Sir Arthur Haselrigg,** of Noseley Hall, Leicestershire, married to Lord Brook's sister and who later became George Fenwick's father-in-law; **John Pym,** Secretary to the Earl of Warwick and leader of the Parliamentary Party in the House of Commons; **John Hampden,** cousin of Oliver Cromwell, imprisoned by Charles I for refusing to pay Ship Money who became an ally of John Pym in the Long Parliament; **Henry Lawrence,** cousin of Oliver Cromwell and President of the Council during the Commonwealth; **John Humphrey; Henry Durley; Sir Richard Knightley, MP** of Fawsley, Northamptonshire; **Sir Thomas Barrington, MP,** friend of Pym and Hampden; **Sir Matthew Boynton** of Barnstone, Yorkshire; **Herbert Pelham** and **Sir Richard Saltonstall.**

John Pym

John Hampden

It is interesting that only these last two Patentees ever travelled to America: Herbert Pelham moved to Boston, Massachusetts and became the first treasurer of Harvard University, while Sir Richard Saltonstall accompanied John Winthrop, the leader of a Puritan clique, to New England in 1629/30. Pelham's daughter Penelope later married one of the sons of John Winthrop the younger.

Chapter III

New England

The Patentees looked for a refuge in New England should events in England put the Puritans in jeopardy. In July 1635 they appointed John Winthrop Junior, then aged 29, whose father was governor in Massachusetts, to be:

"Governor of the river Connecticut in New England and of the Harbours and places adjoininge."

Winthrop had some difficulty in stopping settlers from moving onto the land which he had set aside for the patentees, around the mouth of the river. Many settlers came from the much poorer lands around the Massachusetts coast and they were wanting to settle in this much pleasanter land. He insisted that all Englishmen desiring to settle in the area must obtain their title for the land from the new colony of which he was governor. A lot of them then moved upstream where John Winthrop allowed them to settle provided they accepted his role as their governor. It was soon noted that the area *"presented a curious spectacle of a colony upstream pretending to have a Governor, and a fortified Governor downstream pretending to have a colony!"*

George Fenwick travelled to America as the Agent for the Patentees in 1636. English colonisation in the New World had begun as a purely commercial enterprise with a 1607 Charter granted by James I to the Plymouth Council of New England. Religious dissenters, such as the Pilgrim Fathers in 1620 who sailed to America on the Mayflower, saw the colonies as a chance to create their own religious communities in the New World. It was a few years later that a group of Puritans in England, under the leadership of John Winthrop (1588–1649), set up a Puritan enclave in Massachusetts, disguised as the Massachusetts Bay Company in order to receive Royal Assent. In 1629/30, Winthrop and his group arrived in New England, with Winthrop installed as Governor of Massachusetts. Accompanying Winthrop was Sir Richard Saltonstall, who later founded a township called Watertown, where he lived for a time with his wife and five children. It was his knowledge of the local geography of this part of New England that was to be of great benefit to George Fenwick when Sir Richard left and returned to England in 1634. The 1607 Charter written by James I was couched in very general terms and obviously written with a paucity of geographical knowledge. The Charter granted land to the Warwick Patentees (ie. colonists) from the mouth of the Narrangasset River in the south stretching northwards for 40 leagues (120 miles) and then extending west as a tranche of land *"from the Western Ocean (as the Atlantic was known) in the East to the South Sea (Pacific) in the West."*

Subsequently, it was Sir Richard Saltonstall with his local knowledge who suggested to George Fenwick that the colonisation by the Warwick Patentees should start from Saybrook at the mouth of the Connecticut River. After his arrival in New England in 1636, George signed the Agreement of the Patentees with Governor John Winthrop Senior and then travelled west up Long Island Sound to visit Saybrook. There he met John Winthrop the Younger and Lieutenant Lion Gardiner.

Gardiner had been appointed by the Patentees to construct adequate fortifications around the outpost at Saybrook in order to protect the new colony from Native American marauders. He was a Scottish puritan who had fought in Holland against the Spanish and was then taken on as a specialist Master of fortifications in the Court of the Prince of Orange. He was approached by the Warwick Patentees and agreed to move to Connecticut where he lived at the Fort in Saybrook with his Dutch wife Mary. He organised the necessary fortifications, with two cannon within the palisade on a mound called Fort Hill. and it was here that Mary gave birth to their son David on April 29 1636. David Gardiner was the first white baby to be born on the Connecticut frontier.

George's visit was not a long one. He had brought with him some animal skins and various necessities for living in this isolated spot and promised that more supplies would soon be forthcoming as well as at least two hundred Puritans to help build the fort and surrounding houses. George soon returned to England to report his findings to the Patentees.

At this stage the Connecticut colonies consisted of Hartford, Saybrook and New Haven of which Hartford was the administrative centre. The Rev. Thomas Hooker was Minister of the Hartford congregation. Since Saybrook was a military outpost it was not formally included in the main colony but remained a small colony in its own right.

In 1637 there was increasing trouble with the Pequots, the native inhabitants of Connecticut. They murdered a number of the English settlers and their wives. War was declared on the Pequots in May, and the men of Saybrook, together with volunteers from Massachusetts, fought and beat them decisively in a very bloody battle. They were aided by a group of disaffected native Americans led by Chief Uncas, who had sided with the settlers when thwarted in his bid for leadership of the Pequots. It was the first time that the native inhabitants of the region had experienced European warfare and they were horrified at the way the Pequots were massacred, and the tribe all but wiped out. Soon after that war was over, Lion Gardiner's contract expired as Governor and constructor of the fort at Saybrook and he was happy to end his time at Saybrook as the Patentees had promised much but delivered little. Gardiner bought an island – now called Gardiner Island – in Long Island Sound where his descendants live to this day.

In the mid 1630s, a large number of people from England were emigrating to the New World. It is possible that many of them were looking for an escape route, should the Royalist party gain more control over their lives. Some, like Sir Harry Vane, whose family came from Barnard Castle in

County Durham, and whose father had been Chancellor to Charles I, left England hoping to find religious tolerance. Sir Harry disapproved of the attitude of the Laudian church in England which dictated exactly how people should worship. He came to the colonies of New England with the understanding and blessing of Charles I, planning to stay for three years. He hoped that in the New World people would be allowed to worship as they wished.

Photograph of Statue of Sir Harry Vane (by permission of Boston Public Library)

He was a contemporary of George Fenwick and his statue can be seen in the public library in Boston and shows the dress of the day which George also would have worn. One description of Sir Harry Vane is extremely unflattering:

"If not necessarily cross-eyed, his lopsided face gave that impression; his overlarge chin - accentuated by his plumpness made him seem like a petulant child about to have a tantrum. He always had a harried expression as if evil spirits were pursuing him."

However Vane was *"gracious in manner, grave, pleasing and very accomplished"* and the people of the Massachusetts Bay looked on him as *"a gift from above".* They elected him Governor of Massachusetts Bay Company in 1635 when he was just twenty three years old. During his year in office the University of Harvard was founded in Cambridge, beside Boston, but his tolerant attitude towards religious practice upset the Puritans of the colony. When he defended the right of Anne Hutchinson to express her views on the way the Puritan church was stifling thinking people, especially women, from speaking their minds he lost the support of the Puritan men of Massachusetts and all possibility of being re-elected Governor. He returned home to England and a career with the Parliamentary Party where he achieved a senior role in government and later worked with George Fenwick in Scotland. His life ended on the scaffold after the restoration of Charles II, who described Sir Harry Vane as *"too dangerous a man to let live."*

Meanwhile, on his return to England in 1636, George married Alice, widow of Sir John Boteler of Temton in Kent. Alice's father was Sir Edward Apsley of Worminghurst in Sussex and it was here, close to his wife's family home that the couple initially chose to live. Alice's uncle, Sir Allen Apsley, had been a great enthusiast for the colonisation of New England and had himself served on the Council for New England created by James I. He was also Lord Lieutenant of the Tower of London. Some of his interest in colonisation must have rubbed off on his niece, for Alice was full of ideas and plans for the couple's future together in America. George and Alice made arrangements for their return to America. George mortgaged his land at Brinkburn in Northumberland, and Alice sold her rights to Tote House in Scharnebrooke, Bedfordshire, where she had lived with her first husband. With this money to keep them going they left for America in July 1639, landing at Quillipack in Long Island Sound in a 350 ton ship which had taken seven weeks to cross the Atlantic. It was reported that:

"their passage had been so ordered and their prayers had been accepted, for they had no illness in the ship, apart from a little sea sickness."

This ship, which was reputed to be called 'Fair Haven', succeeded in entering the harbour without the need for a pilot, steered *"by God's own hand."* It was thought to be the first ship from London to dock there and as a result of that satisfactory voyage the town was re-named New Haven.

George had signed the agreement of the Patentees with John Winthrop Senior in 1636 on his first visit to Connecticut. By the time of his second visit he was not only acting as Agent to the Patentees but had also become one of their number. He was appointed Governor of Saybrook by John Winthrop Junior in 1639 and came to live at the Fort in Saybrook bringing with him his wife Alice, their infant son Edward, and also two of his sisters from Brinkburn, Mary and Elizabeth. In 1640 their daughter Elizabeth was born and was baptised by Rev.Thomas Hooker in Hartford, where the family were accepted and became part of the congregation.

Alice as the widow of Sir John Boteler, who had died in 1634, became known incorrectly as 'Lady' Alice. She was described *"as a stately young woman, beautiful, golden-haired, and of a gracious presence and a graceful manner."* She has been called the First Lady of Connecticut, although others such as Ella T. Grasso 1919-1968, the first female governor of Connecticut, and "Goody" Barber the first white woman to set foot on dry land in Connecticut in 1635 vie for that title, not to mention Lion Gardner's wife, who, as we have seen, gave birth to the first white child in Connecticut at the fort in Saybrook. Alice was very well liked and a huge support to her husband in those early settlement days. It is said that the pedigree of a herd of cows in Westbrook descends from the cows brought over to the New World by Alice.

Fort Saybrook   *Painting by Peter Langley*

The Fenwick family lived in the fort at Saybrook, originally constructed under the direction of Lion Gardiner, looking out onto Long Island Sound from the west bank at the mouth of the Connecticut River. George became engrossed with the affairs of the colony at the same time amassing a large estate around Saybrook. The family settled into daily life, attended by a native American servant called Obed. George wrote to a friend in England describing the life of a pioneer in a new land:

"We both delight in that primitive employment of dressing a garden … I am well stored with apple and cherry trees though worms have destroyed many. My wife cultivates flowers and herbs, keeps pet rabbits and hunts for game with her shooting gun."

A lawyer and a soldier, Colonel George, as he became known, was greatly involved in the scheme for colonising Connecticut. He and his family found life at the fort stimulating and very pleasant. In addition to his wife, children and his two sisters living at the fort, he had also his chaplain, Mr Peters, and Surgeon Pell. John Winthrop Junior, who had learnt some medicine whilst at Trinity College, Dublin, advised Lady Alice on what to plant in her herb garden and how to use the herbs.

She grew St John's Wort, used for treating vertigo, epilepsy and madness; elderberry for wines and wounds especially gunshot wounds; and rhubarb and bryony for cathartics. Winthrop also had a prescription from *'the best London physician'* for the treatment of *"plagues, smallpox, agues, purples and any form of fever, poisons and the King's Evil".* This was a concoction of black powder, of which the basic ingredient was pulverized burnt toads. Lady Alice was also advised to keep bullet- shaped pills containing maidenhead fern, fennel, parsley root, two or three ounces of almond oil and one quarter pound of fresh butter as a treatment for many common ailments.

As the years intervened it became clear to the original Warwick Patentees that the colonies were not going to support an aristocracy on the English model. As a result the two main sponsors of the Warwick Patent, Lord Saye and Sele and Lord Brooke, began to lose interest in the development of the colony and Colonel George realised that it was most unlikely that any of his co-Patentees would come out to Connecticut, build houses and settle in the area he had allotted to them. His personal estate had grown considerably, and he allowed the citizens of Saybrook to have the use of the Western neck of ground outside Saybrook for their animals, though reserving to himself *"the property notwithstanding".* So, even in those early days, much of the area was used as a common but within limits.

This is the ground now called the Borough of Fenwick, Old Saybrook. Colonel George represented Connecticut at the meeting of the Commissioners of the United Colonies, held in Boston in 1643. He had long desired and advocated a union of all the local colonies and worked hard for this cause. Then, at a crucial stage in his negotiations, disaster struck: his wife Alice died, probably from a puerperal fever following the birth of their second daughter, Dorothy in 1644. Lady Alice was buried at the fort where she had died and George arranged for her grave to be looked after by Matthew Griswold, one of the oldest settlers in Old Lyme, on the other side of the Connecticut River.

In 1870, two hundred and twenty five years later, when the railroad was due to be built through the original fort, a reburial of Lady Alice Fenwick was arranged. With great state and ceremony her remains were exhumed, medically examined and a lock of her hair kept as a memento. This can still be seen in the Hart House in Old Saybrook. The service of reburial on November 23, 1870, in the Congregational Church was noteworthy and was attended by approximately 300 people: numerous eminent historians spoke. Her coffin was then escorted to the accompaniment of muffled drums and the tolling of church bells of both the Saybrook churches, to a burial place of honour in the New Burial Ground. Her grave is still tended here.

Lady Alice Fenwick's grave (Photograph by Bob Czepiel)

Colonel George Fenwick was devastated by his wife's death. His married idyll at Saybrook destroyed, he pursued his idea of a united colony of Connecticut with renewed vigour. He sold the fort and its appurtenances, together with all those lands in the independent colony of Saybrook, claimed by the Warwick Patent, to the Colony of Connecticut for £1600.

Lady Alice Fenwick had been a renowned figure in Connecticut and was immortalised in a "Hesitation Waltz" which was published in the early 20th Century.

Having brought about the unification for which he had been striving, George returned home to England. At the same time, he pledged that all the land mentioned in the patents should fall under the jurisdiction of the Colony of Connecticut, should this be within his power.

In the years that followed this was to be the cause of numerous disputes with the Colony, to the extent that in 1657, the year following George's death, the authorities refused to release his estate to his heirs until they had paid the Colony £500 for the non-fulfillment of that original pledge. George must have realized the likelihood of this occurrence as in his Will he left exactly such a sum *"to the public use of that country of New England, if my loving friend Edward Hopkins thinks fit".* At the time of his departure he gave to the newly united colony of Connecticut its seal, consisting of fifteen vines, supported and bearing fruit and representing the fifteen supporters of the Warwick patent. A hand above the vines comes out of the clouds and carries a label with the motto *"Sustinet qui transtulit"* which translates as *"He who transplanted continues to sustain".* The current seal of Connecticut looks rather different with only three vines, which are said to represent the original three colonies of Hartford, New Haven and Saybrook. The meaning of the motto was explained in a letter stamped in Weathersfeld, Connecticut, on April 23rd 1775 which says:

"We fix on our standards and drums the colony arms with the motto 'Qui transtulit sustinet' round them in letters of gold which we construe thus: God, who transplanted us hither, will support us."

The 80th Psalm is a possible source for this motto:

"thou hast brought a vine out of Egypt, thou has cast out the heathen and planted it."

At a later stage in the Seventeenth Century Saybrook became the home of a College of further education, which was later incorporated into Yale University when it was founded in 1701, This College moved to New Haven taking with it the emblem, a seal taken from the Coat of Arms of the Fiennes family of Saye and Sele.

Yale University Stone in Old Saybrook

One of the colleges at Yale University is now known as Saybrook College. Although it was founded in 1933, its students commemorate Lord Saye and Sele and Lord Brook as its 'step-founders' with a birthday celebration held each year on a weekend in late spring. The badge of the College is the grapevine, which is derived from the original seal of Saybrook Colony and can be seen carved in stone over the High Street gate to the college. George retained extensive amounts of land as well as the taxes from the export of corn, cattle, bacon and biscuits from the Connecticut river for ten years after he left the Colony. Much later on his death in 1656 he bequeathed his large estates in and around Saybrook to his sister Elizabeth, who in 1648 had married Captain John Cullick, Secretary of the Colony. She and her husband remained at Saybrook until Cullick's death in 1683, after which she married Richard Eley of Boston. She is buried in the Eley family burial ground outside Old Lyme. In his will, Colonel George also bequeathed four acres of land in Saybrook to *"my faithful servant, Obed"*.

Chapter IV

Civil War

George travelled home to Brinkburn with his baby daughter. His other sister, Mary, followed with his son, Edward, and his older daughter Elizabeth. As this letter to John Winthrop the Younger shows, they had to wait some time before they were able to leave Boston.

From: Winthrop Papars, Mass. Hist. Coll.; Copied from loose copies at the Stevenson Archive Building, Old Saybrook, 8 Mar. 2001. Letter to John Winthrop, Jr. from Mary Fenwick at Saybrook, 6 July, 1646.

MARY FFENWICK TO JOHN WINTHROP, JR.

To my honoored freind mr. John winthrop at his house Ten hills in Mattachusetts Bay these present

SIR, Mr. Peters hath broke open tha shall you sent me and I have tasted of the Curnell, which affected me a treble sweet, first a relish of your affectionate care, speedily to convey it by such safe hands; secondly an hearty refreshment of my spitits upon the suruein of my brothers safety in England and his tender love reflected upon his and my selfe in this country; lastly his commands of my presence with him in the land of our nativity, in the strength of these juices I shall walke and wait a while heere, till your continued watch return me answers when and how I and My Nephew and Neece may be accommodated in some one of those ships that are com ?????????ing into Boston, on hope of which I shall hartily feed, till I set my feet aborde the vessell. In the maane and ever, heare or in England be pleased to present my services to your good wife, and my sisters to you both.

SEABROOKE, 6 Julie 1646

This letter refers to her nephew and niece, Edward and Elisabeth Fenwick, who are to go back to England with her. The little sister, Dorothy, has already or is to go back with the nurse, either with George Fenwick, or on another ship. What we do not know is if Edward survived the trip, or perhaps died later, in England. We do know that his Uncle Edward Fenwick's will which had left his estate to the boy was eventually changed. George Fenwick had originally been named as guardian to Edward's inheritance until he became of age. Where can we find the story of the next few years - back in England?

Mary went on to marry Thomas Legard, Mayor of Newcastle. Nothing more is known of Edward. In her last years Mary Legard lived with her cousin Robert Hazlerigg at Swarland Old Hall and in his will he left her rooms there where she could live out her life. He also left his estate at Swarland to his cousin Sir Robert Hazlerigg of Noseley, who was the younger son of Sir Arthur. The grave of Sir Robert of Swarland can still be found in a field behind Swarland Old Hall. Alice's uncle, Edward Apsley, left his land in Sussex to his nephew Edward on the understanding that he would change his name from Fenwick to Apsley on reaching the age of twenty-one and gaining his inheritance: it seems likely that he died before reaching his majority.

Because George owned the land at Brinkburn he was eligible to stand for Parliament, and in 1645 he was elected by the people of Morpeth to sit as their Member in the Long Parliament. His immediate predecessors as Members for Morpeth had been Sir William Carnaby and John Fenwick, son of Sir John Fenwick of Wallington. Both these were Royalists. Given their allegiance to Charles I and their perceived misdeeds against Parliament they were excluded from sitting and voting in the Long Parliament. Shortly after this John Fenwick was killed, fighting for the King at the Battle of Marston Moor. This often occurs during a Civil War when neighbours and families find themselves fighting on opposite sides.

As a result of his military experiences in America, George was given permission not to sit continuously in Parliament. He became one of the Commissioners for the Plantation of America and Commissioner for securing Peace with Scotland. In 1647 he served in the New Model Army in Ireland and then did great service for the Roundhead cause by capturing a large number of the Royalists in Northumberland after the Royalists had captured Berwick on Tweed. In 1648 he had a 'gallant victory' defeating Langdale's forces under Sir Richard Tempest, going on to relieve Holy Island and storming and recapturing Fenham Castle.

George was appointed Governor of Berwick in 1649 after the town's surrender to the Roundheads and he soon became a great benefactor.

Under his direction a Church was built by a mason from London, one John Young of Blackfriars. Fenwick's Regiment of Foot Soldiers did much of the work, removing stone from the castle on the

Berwick-upon-Tweed Bridge

other side of the town for the new church. The castle had been built in the Twelfth Century by Edward I. George raised money for the Church building by applying to the government in London for funds to support the inhabitants in food. He claimed that the Scots were likely to lay siege to the town. Berwick had been besieged more times than any other town apart from Jerusalem, so that this claim for funds would have seemed very sensible. However no such siege took place and the money provided was used to build the Church. He succeeded in reducing the excise duty paid by the inhabitants, including the abolition of duty on beer and malt

Berwick Parish Church

spirit, which according to his plea to parliament was:

"impoverishing the inhabitants. If they get drink for their families and grain for their cattle free from duty they will think themselves well."

George became a very popular governor perhaps as a result of this. It was a rare thing in those days when a garrison of soldiers and their Governor were seen as a drain on the community and its resources.

Chapter V

The Battle of Dunbar

Oliver Cromwell

In July 1650, as Governor of Berwick, Colonel George Fenwick received Oliver Cromwell when he came north on his way to Edinburgh. It was Cromwell's decision to make the port of Dunbar, a few miles north of Berwick, the supply base for his military campaign. From here the New Model Army, led by Cromwell advanced towards Edinburgh, but sickness amongst his troops forced him to retreat from Musselburgh back to Dunbar. He was pursued by General Leslie, the Scottish general who led a much larger force of 14,000 soldiers as compared to the New Model Army of 11,000.

Colonel George Fenwick commanded his Berwick garrison regiment of foot soldiers, and this now became part of Cromwell's New Model Army. At the same time, Sir Arthur Haselrigg, the Governor of Newcastle and an old friend of Cromwell, and who had also been one of the Patentees of Connecticut, commanded another garrison Regiment of Foot Soldiers. George had married for the second time, to Catherine, the daughter of Sir Arthur. Although more than thirty years younger than her husband, this marriage forged a strong link between these two families and their regiments. Both garrison regiments contained many experienced soldiers. Cromwell was keen to make use of General George Monck, an ex-Royalist, who had fought well for the Roundheads in Ulster. Cromwell decided to amalgamate five companies from each of Fenwick and Hazelrigg's regiments under the command of General Monck, who named the regiment The Coldstream Regiment.

The new regiment played a prominent part in winning the battle of Dunbar, where they occupied the centre of the field against a superior number of Scots under General Leslie.

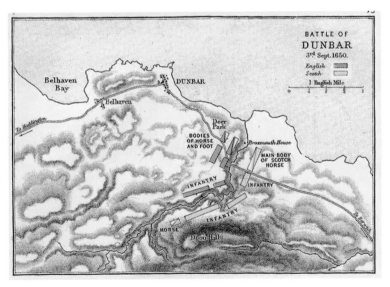

Disposition of troops before the battle

THE BATTLE OF DUNBAR

The strategy of the battle fought in early September 1650 showed the brilliance of Cromwell as a General, but was also influenced by the fact that Leslie was hamstrung by the Committee of Estates of The Kirk. These worthies insisted on coming into his army camp from Edinburgh and removing those officers and men who did not comply with their rigorous catechisms on Old Testament history. In a very short time this move reduced his force by eighty officers and about three thousand men, although the Scots still remained larger than the English army. The Committee of Estates of The Kirk also insisted that they should have a say in the running of the battle, which caused great dissention in the Scottish Council of War. Although the Committee of Estates were against any fighting on The Lord's Day the Scots army would have had a better chance of beating Cromwell had they fought the battle on Sunday, September 1st, the day that Cromwell reached Dunbar. The Estates were also determined to fight according to the Old Testament books of Joshua and Judges, and persuaded Leslie to lead his army down from Doon Hill on which he was camped, as both Gideon and Ehud had done in biblical times. Both armies, full of religous vigour, called upon the Almighty for help. To paraphrase Winston Churchill from The History of The English Speaking Peoples:

"The Lord, in His infinite wisdom, decided to ignore all calls for divine intervention and relied on the military capabilities of both armies to battle it out."

The English were amazed to see the Scots moving off the hill late on Monday afternoon and Cromwell, realising that the Scots were likely to attack in the morning, decided to pre-empt them by attacking before dawn. Cromwell's men were close to the shore with their backs to the sea, in a place which would be difficult to defend. During the stormy night when the noise of the surf and waves drowned the sound, Cromwell moved his cavalry to the left flank of his army so that he could attack the unprotected right wing of the Scots. The Scots were unaware of what was afoot. Many of the Scottish officers left their men to go and find shelter from the storm.

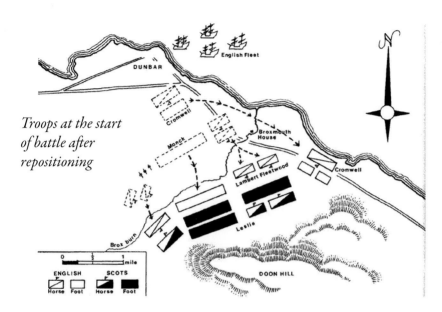

Troops at the start of battle after repositioning

At about 4.00 a.m. the English artillery opened fire and the foot soldiers advanced on the Scots. They were repulsed by the Scottish pikemen, renowned to be the best in Europe, and the cavalry was also put under pressure. Whilst this frontal assault was going on, Cromwell brought in the main Ironsides cavalry (so nicknamed by the Royalists as it seemed to cut through it's enemies with ease), situated opposite the right flank of the Scots army, charging at them from the side. This caused huge consternation in the Scottish ranks. As the Scottish right wing fell back towards the centre, it blocked their own movements and when the remaining English cavalry with the New Model Army, including Monck's regiment, attacked again, the Scottish centre collapsed in chaos. Hemmed in by the hill above and behind them, the left wing of the Scottish army were unable to engage with the enemy, and fled the field. The Coldstream regiment together with the rest of the New Model Army turned the battle into a rout and the Scottish army became a shambles, as the English sensed victory.

Two hours after it started the battle was over. A great number of the Scottish army never came into action and could do nothing but flee. As they left the battlefield they would have heard the sound of the victorious English soldiers singing Psalm 17, which psalm they themselves had been practising to sing had they been victorious. It includes the verse:

"Arise O Lord, stand in their way and cast them down;
deliver me from the wicked by your sword."

Chapter VI

The Formation of the Coldstream Guards

Fenwick's and Haselrigg's Regiments under the command of Colonel Monck had done well, and they remained as the Coldstream Guards, the oldest existing British Regiment of Foot Guards.

Guardsmen have boots with 13 studs in them, one for each of the members of the regiment who have won the Victoria Cross

Ten years later in 1660, this Regiment marched from Coldstream under the command of General Monck, to restore Charles II to the English throne. The foot guards marched to London and were billeted in St. James Palace where they behaved well and greatly impressed the citizens of London. In 1661 they marched to Tower Hill, the last regiment to be disbanded after the Civil War. They were given the order to lay down their arms which they did immediately. They were then ordered to take them up as the Second Regiment of Foot. They refused to do so, saying they were *"second to none."* This is the derivation of the regimental motto *"Nulli Secundus"* . After rapid consultation amongst the senior officers, the order was rescinded and a new order was given that they should take up their arms as the Lord General's First Regiment of Foot Guards, an order with which they complied. Their commanding Officer, General Monck went on to become the Duke of Albemarle.

From 1670, General Monck's Regiment of Foot was known as the Coldstream Regiment of Foot Guards, and later as The Coldstream Guards in honour of the march from Coldstream to London which brought about the Restoration. It is in proud recognition of the contribution made by Colonel George Fenwick and Sir Arthur Haselrigg, the co-founders of the Coldstream Guards that this Regiment remains the oldest regular Regiment in continuous service in the British Army today and abides as:

"the one complete relic of the famous New Model Army."

I have mentioned the religous zeal of some of the soldiers of both armies; and give an example of the extreme attitudes often taken in such circumstances. A Yorkshireman, James Naylor, suffered dreadfully for his religious beliefs. He fought in the New Model Army and was also a very fiery preacher. One of Cromwell's officers said that he was more frightened by Naylor's sermon than by the imminent battle.

Naylor's followers believed his extreme views and were convinced that he was a reincarnation of Jesus Christ. He was so encouraged by them after

Dunbar that he changed his name from James to Jesus. When Cromwell heard of this he arrested him and had him tried and found guilty of blasphemy. As a result Naylor was whipped and pilloried in London before having a red-hot bolt put into his tongue and a letter B branded on his forehead –- standing for *'blasphemer'.* He was then sent to prison in Bristol for two years where the punishment was repeated. He refused the aid of any doctor, saying that God was his physician and he needed no other. On discharge from prison, he planned a return to Yorkshire but on his way he was attacked by highwaymen who injured him so badly that he died shortly after. An unfortunate end to a dramatic story of bigotry but one that shows Cromwell's determination to counter the effects of such blasphemers.

The Coldstream Guards have continued their links with Berwick upon Tweed. At the time of the closure of Berwick upon Tweed Borough Council in 2009 the regiment marched through the town wearing their bearskins and looking magnificent with the regimental band playing various Northumbrian tunes. Amongst those present to witness the event was Lord Ridley who had joined the regiment 66 years earlier and fought with them from the Normandy beaches across Europe into Germany. He is pictured under George Fenwick's memorial beside Canon Alan Hughes, the vicar of Berwick, Major Crofton and Lieutenant Colonel Vernon.

Chapter VII

The Last Years

Edinburgh Castle

After the Battle of Dunbar George Fenwick continued on into Scotland with Cromwell taking part in the siege of Edinburgh Castle, which continued until Christmas 1650 before the Scots capitulated, and Colonel Walter Dundas of That Ilk, the Governor, surrendered.

During the siege Cromwell had a prolonged bout of ill health. It is interesting to speculate whether George ever contemplated asking advice from Doctor Claudius, his younger brother, who was now qualified and practising medicine in Newcastle, where George's father-in-law was commanding the garrison. As a reward for George's success in the siege, he was made Governor of Edinburgh Castle. This is one of the oldest titles in Scotland and one of which the Scots are extremely proud.

A local historian reported that the fortress was then garrisoned with *"English blasphemers under Colonel Fenwick."* There is a board in Edinburgh Castle which lists all the Castle Governors since Roger de Stuteville in 1177. The name of George Fenwick is not on it, although he is clearly shown to have been the Governor on a list held by the Governor.

Perhaps the Scots would argue that these English Governors were not appointed by a reigning Monarch and were therefore inferior and not worthy of recognition. George Fenwick was the first Englishman to hold the post and was certainly very proud of the honour. This 'airbrushing' of the first Englishman, who could at a stretch even be described as the only American ever to hold this ancient title is an interesting reaction by Scottish historians to the defeat of their army by Oliver Cromwell. Even more fascinating is the fact that history is usually written by the victors, but, as demonstrated on this occasion, as on numerous others, the Scots used their experience in writing history from the vanquished point of view. George had held the post by conquest, first at the Battle of Dunbar, and then by the siege of Edinburgh Castle itself, so was no doubt doubly unpopular with the Scots.

On his return to England George was given the freedom of the City of Newcastle where his father-in-law was Governor, his sister's husband had just been Mayor and his brother Claudius was now practising medicine. He was made one of the Commissioners sent into Scotland by the English government. The Commissioners aimed to redress grievances and settle outstanding disputes, in the hope of an Act of Union between the two countries. His fellow Commissioners were Sir Harry Vane from Massachusetts, Chief Justice St John and General Monck. Although they worked hard to introduce a Bill in Parliament to provide such an Act, it was another fifty years before the Union became a fact.

At the end of the Long Parliament, George lost his seat and did not sit in the Barebones Parliament in 1653 at the beginning of the Commonwealth. He was not considered to be sufficiently supportive of Cromwell as he had not been wholeheartedly in favour of executing Charles I. It is interesting that in 1649 George had been appointed one of the Commissioners for the trial of the King but he did not take any part in the proceedings. George later returned to Parliament as the Member for Berwick in 1654 and again in 1656. At that time he was described as being "Governor of the Garrison at Leith and Edinburgh" as well as Governor of Berwick. He and his wife Catherine continued to reside in Berwick, close to the Church which he had been instrumental in building, one of only two built in England during the Commonwealth. This lovely Church is of great architectural interest as it has neither tower nor spire. Cromwell did not think such additions seemly. The citizens of Berwick gave George a great send-off when he travelled south to London for the beginning of the 1656 Parliament: he never returned, dying on March 15th, 1656 at his estate at Worminghurst, Sussex, where he stayed when attending Parliament. He had inherited Worminghurst from his first wife's family and is buried there.

Had Colonel George lived into the time of the Restoration, it is likely that he would have suffered the fate of the previous owners of Brinkburn Priory. His friend Sir Arthur Haselrigg died in the Tower and his contemporary, Sir Harry Vane had his head cut off. With the history of George's links with the Parliamentary Party he would undoubtedly have been executed as well, thereby continuing the sequence of death by beheading suffered by the early owners of Brinkburn. As it was, the citizens of Berwick-upon-Tweed erected a memorial in the Church dedicated to him which reads:

Col. George Fenwick
of Brinkburn, Esq
Governor of Berwick in the year 1652
was a principal instrument of causing
this Church to be built, and died
March 15th 1656
A GOOD MAN IS A PUBLIC GOOD

The eloquence of that simple statement at the end of his memorial sums up the way that Puritan England saw its heroes. None of the later flowery prose of the eighteenth century; just a simple statement of fact, itself like the Commonwealth Churches with no outward show. Here was a dignified record of the life of a man who did more in his fifty three years than most of his contemporaries, who lived much longer. I know of no-one else who not only founded a Colony, a Church and a Regiment, but was also linked to the founding of a University as well as being the first English Governor of Edinburgh Castle. I believe he deserves the accolade of being a Great Founding Father.

He left his estate at Worminghurst to both his daughters, his son Edward having died. The elder daughter Elizabeth had married Sir Thomas Hazelrigg of Noseley, Leicestershire. He was the son of Sir Arthur Hazelrigg, George's friend and co-founder of the Coldstream Guards. Thomas therefore was also the brother of George's second wife Catherine; an interesting, yet quite complex, relationship. The younger daughter, Dorothy, had married Sir Thomas Williams of East Markham.

The two sisters shared the estate at Worminghurst for about ten years and then sold it to Mr. Henry Bigland who, by a curious twist of fate, sold it to William Penn, the Quaker who went on to found the colony of Pennsylvania. There is a feeling that the house at Worminghurst must have held some very special colonising energy. First there was Sir Allen Apsley on the Council for New England; then there was Alice and her husband George; finally, out of the blue, comes William Penn, the founder and "Absolute Proprietor" of the province of Pennsylvania which in time became the state of Pennsylvania. On moving to America, Penn sold the house to John Butler, who pulled it down and built a new one.

William Penn

George's widow Catherine, returned to Northumberland and married as her second husband, Colonel Philip Babington. He was related to Anthony Babington who in 1586 had plotted to put Mary Queen of Scots on the English throne. Colonel Philip Babington took over the Governorship of Berwick after George Fenwick died, and then married George's widow. Catherine was an extremely forceful woman with very strong puritanical views and she 'fell out' with the vicar when she was living at Harnham in the Parish of Bolam, in central Northumberland. She carried her antagonism to great extremes and arranged with the local blacksmith to come into the church at Bolam, during the Sunday service, while the vicar was preaching, and throw him physically out of his church. This dramatic incident duly took place, greatly to the consternation of both the vicar and the remainder of the congregation.

Bolam Church

The resulting furore was considerable and Catherine Babington was excommunicated from the Church. Consequently she was not entitled to be buried in consecrated ground when she died on August 28, 1670. The vicar, Rev. Forster of Bolam, refused to bury her anywhere, let alone at Bolam, as he was still smarting at the indignity she had perpetrated upon him. The understandable intransigence of the vicar in denying her this Last Rite, meant that her coffin was placed in a tomb carved out of the rock in the quarry at Harnham, on September 9th, 1670. This area has since been known as the Tomb Garden. She has remained unburied ever since and still lies in the quarry. The tomb was once vandalised by gypsies and to protect it the owner, Mr Wake, had it covered in concrete where it remains as a constant reminder of the strength of opposing religious views which existed in the Seventeenth Century. The present owner feels that the quarry is dangerous and does not allow anyone to visit it. Thus one of George Fenwick's wives was buried twice and the other has not been buried at all. Another remarkable coincidence!

In his Will, George bequeathed the land at Brinkburn and Longfram-lington to his brother Dr Claudius Fenwick. This was the beginning of the medical links with Brinkburn and Longframlington that continue to the present day.

Postscript

I am in the throes of writing "Medicine in the Blood," a history of my medical family, and hope it will be published in the near future. In it you will come across some different characters, many of whom have no direct link with the medical profession. There are border reivers; a botanising clergyman who was also a doctor; an international rugby player; a manufacturer of soap; a master of foxhounds; an enthusiastic farmer who was one of the first to use steam- ploughing successfully; the Colonel of a volunteer regiment of soldiers; an itinerant preacher; the shorthand writer in parliament who was present on the day the Prime Minister was assassinated; the first man to cross the High Level bridge over the Tyne; a shale miner from Whitby; the writer of "The Lambton Worm"; a man whose wife bore him twenty- six children; the chairman of the Royal Commission which looked into the control of Foot and Mouth Disease; and a potential regicide who failed but whose horse succeeded. As well as all these characters there is also the family and social history of eight generations of doctors, starting with George's brother Claudius. All the doctors are linked in some way to the village of Longframlington in central Northumberland, where I now live.

I hope these dramatis personae will whet your appetite to explore the book. It is the story of my Northumbrian clan who, for the last four hundred years, can boast of having a doctor in the family, and medicine in the blood.

March 2009.

Chronological Index

1135 Founding of Brinkburn Priory, in the parish of Longframlington, Northumberland.

1533 Henry VIII annuls his marriage to Catherine of Aragon in order that he may marry Anne Boleyn. Their daughter Mary loses her position as legitimate heir.

1533 Anne Boleyn gives birth to Elizabeth, the heiress presumptive to the English throne but not the male heir whom Henry VIII craves to secure the Tudor succession.

1536 Anne Boleyn beheaded and Elizabeth, her daughter declared illegitimate and deprived of the title of princess.

1536 Eleven days after Anne Boleyn's death, Henry marries Jane Seymour who dies shortly after the birth of their son, Prince Edward.

1536 Visitation from Henry VIII's Commissioners, Drs Layton and Legh to Brinkburn Priory

1536 Under the Act of Dissolution the Priory is dissolved

1537 The Pilgrimage if Grace, a rebellion by the Catholic gentry of England in protest against HenryVIII's break with Rome and the Dissolution of the Monasteries in which Sir Thomas Percy is attainted and later executed for his involvement.

1543 Succession to the Crown Act

1546 Brinkburn Priory leased to George Fenwick, by John Dudley, the Earl of Warwick, later to become the Duke of Northumberland

1547 Death of Henry VIII and ascension of the "Boy King" Edward VI, age 9

1547 Edward Seymour, the Duke of Somerset and the new King's eldest Uncle, rules as Protector

1549 The introduction of The Book of Common Prayer (replaces Latin services with English). Church of England becomes more explicitly Protestant.

1551 Duke of Somerset overthrown by the Duke of Northumberland, who assumes role as Protector

1552 Duke of Somerset executed

1552 Duke of Northumberland marries his son, Lord Guildford Dudley to Lady Jane Grey, one of Henry VIII's great-nieces and a claimant to the throne.

1553 Edward VI sweeps aside Succession to the Crown Act, excluding both Mary and Elizabeth and accepts Jane as his heir. On his death, Jane assumes the throne and is accepted by the Council.

1553 The country rallies to Mary, Catherine of Aragon's daughter and a devout Roman Catholic. Jane reigns for only nine days.

1553 Mary is crowned with her half-sister, Elizabeth at her side and becomes the first Queen Regnant (a queen reigning in her own right rather than a queen through marriage to a king).

1554 Lady Jane Grey and her husband are executed.

1554 Mary restores papal supremacy in England, reintroduces Roman Catholic bishops and begins the slow reintroduction of monastic orders. She also revives the old heresy laws to secure the religious conversion of the country. Around 300 Protestant heretics are burnt at the stake including Thomas Cranmer (a former Protestant archbishop and author of two common books of prayer).

1554 Mary I marries Philip, King of Spain from 1556. The marriage is deeply unpopular with Parliament and drags England into war with Spain against France.

1554 Wyatt's Rebellion. . Uprisings break out in several parts of England and Wales, led by Thomas Wyatt. Upon their collapse Elizabeth is interrogated and imprisoned in the Tower of London and held under house arrest for the next year.

1555 Elizabeth is recalled to court

1557 Mary gives the land previously held by the Duke of Northumberland to Thomas Percy,

1558 Mary dies childless leaving the Crown to her half sister, Elizabeth.
1558 George Fenwick assigns his lease of Brinkburn to his younger
brother Tristram, the land of which is now owned by Thomas, Earl of
Northumberland.
1558 Elizabeth accedes to the throne.
1559 The new Queen establishes a secure Church of England, a
compromise between Roman Catholicism and Protestantism. The new
Act of Supremacy becomes law whereby all public officials swear an oath
of loyalty to the monarch as the supreme governor of the Church of
England or risk disqualification from office; the heresy laws are repealed,
to avoid a repeat of the persecution of dissenters practised by Mary.
1559 Act of Uniformity is passed, which makes attendance at church
and the use of an adapted version of the 1552 Book of Common Prayer
compulsory, though the penalties for recusancy, or failure to attend and
conform, are not extreme.
1560 Treaty of Edinburgh is signed following English aid to Scottish
Protestant rebels, successfully removing the French Catholic threat in
the north.
1561 Mary, Queen of Scots leaves France and returns to Scotland
to rule. In contrast to her Catholic upbringing, Scotland has an
established Protestant church and is run by a council of Protestant
nobles supported by Elizabeth.
1567 Shortly after the death of her first husband, Darnley, Mary marries
the Earl of Bothwell, believed to have been a conspirator in Darnley's
death. Mary is forced to abdicate by the Scottish lords, in favour of
her son James, born in 1566, who is bought up as a Protestant. Mary
escapes to England where she is imprisoned by Elizabeth, her cousin,
for the next 19 years.
1569 The Rising of the North, in which both Thomas Percy and
Tristram Fenwick participate and are captured,
1586 Babington Plot by Catholic rebels to replace Elizabeth with Mary

as Queen of England, prompts Elizabeth to sign Mary's death warrant.
1587 Mary, Queen of Scots is beheaded in Northamptonshire.
1588 Defeat of the Spanish Armada
1594 - 1603, Elizabeth battles with the Irish Catholics in the Nine Years
War. Ireland surrenders a few days after her death.
Expeditions of discovery, by Francis Drake, Walter Raleigh and
Humphrey Gilbert, particularly to the Americas, prepare England for
an age of colonisation and trade expansion. The Colony of Virginia is
named after Queen Elizabeth
1603 On Elizabeth's death, King James VI of Scotland, son of Mary
Queen of Scotts, succeeds Elizabeth as King James I of England and
Ireland. He rules England, Scotland and Ireland often using the title
King of Great Britain.
1603 Birth of Colonel George Fenwick who is to grow up living at
Brinkburn with his brothers and sisters.
1604 The commissioning of a new translation and compilation of
approved books of the Bible to confirm the divine right of kings to rule,
which becomes known as the King James Bible, and is completed in
1611.
1605 Gunpowder Plot aimed to blow up the Houses of Parliament.
1614 –21 After repeated conflicts with Parliament, James I rules
without Parliament employing officials, who are astute at raising and
saving money for the crown, and selling earldoms and other dignities,
many created for the purpose, as an alternative source of income.
1620 Departure of the Mayflower from Southampton carrying the
Pilgrim Fathers , the name applied to the early settlers of the Plymouth
Colony in present-day Plymouth, Massachusetts.
1625 Death of James I and the accession of his son, King Charles I,
to whom James bequeathes a fatal belief in the divine right of kings,
combined with a disdain for Parliament.
1625 Charles is married by proxy to Henrietta Maria of France. Many

members of Parliament are opposed to his marriage to a Roman Catholic, fearing that Charles will lift restrictions on Roman Catholics and undermine the official establishment of Protestantism.

1626 George Fenwick buys back the land at Brinkburn.

1628 Parliament adopts a Petition of Right, calling upon the King to acknowledge that he cannot levy taxes without Parliament's consent, impose martial law on civilians, imprison them without due process, or quarter troops in their homes. Charles assents to the petition, though he continues to claim the right to collect customs duties without authorization from Parliament.

1633 Appointment of William Laud as Archbishop of Canterbury who starts a series of unpopular reforms in an attempt to impose order and authority on the church. Laud attempts to ensure religious uniformity by dismissing non-conformist clergymen and closing Puritan organizations. This is actively hostile to the Reformed tendencies of many of his English and Scottish subjects. To punish those who refuse to accept his reforms, Laud uses the most arbitrary courts in the land, the Court of High Commission and the Court of the Star Chamber.

1634 Reintroduction of an obsolete feudal tax known as ship money, previously only authorized during wars. Charles, however, seeks to collect the tax during peacetime which proves increasingly unpopular with the ruling classes.

1638 The General Assembly of the Church of Scotland abolish Episcopalian government (governance of the Church by bishops) replacing it with Presbyterian government (governance by elders and deacons), Charles seeks to put down what he sees as a rebellion against his authority.

1639 George and Alice Fenwick set sail to America, George now appointed as the fifteenth member of the Warwick Patentees.

1639 The First Bishops' War in Scotland breaks out. It ends in humiliating defeat for Charles.

1640 Charles's military failure in the First Bishops' War causes a financial and military crisis. Charles is forced to end his Personal Rule and recall Parliament into session in an attempt to raise funds. An impasse is reached when Parliament demands the discussion of various abuses of power during the Personal Rule. Both sides refuse to give ground on this matter and, Parliament is dissolved in May 1640, less than a month after it assembles; the Parliament becomes known as the "Short Parliament".

1640 Second Bishops War requires Charles to pay the expenses of his own Scottish army. Charles summons another Parliament in November, which, becomes known as the Long Parliament and is led by John Pym.

1641 To prevent the King from dissolving it at will, Parliament passes the Triennial Act which requires that Parliament is to be summoned at least once every three years, and that when the King fails to issue proper summons, the members can assemble on their own; subsequently that Parliament cannot be dissoved without its own consent. More concessions follow including the abolition of the Court of High Commission and the Star Chamber.

1641 The House of Commons passes the Grand Remonstrance, a long list of grievances against actions by Charles' ministers that are asserted to be abuses of royal power that Charles has committed since the beginning of his reign.

Charles enters the House of Commons with an armed force on 4 January 1642, but finds that his opponents have already escaped, with the exception of Oliver Cromwell. He asks the Speaker, William Lenthall, where the MPs have fled, and Lenthall famously replies, "May it please your Majesty, I have neither eyes to see nor tongue to speak in this place but as the House is pleased to direct me, whose servant I am here." This move is politically disastrous for Charles. It causes acute embarrassment for the monarch and essentially triggers the total breakdown of government in England. Afterwards, Charles can no longer feel safe in London and he begins travelling north to raise an army against Parliament;

1642 The Civil War starts with the inconclusive Battle of Edgehill and continues indescisively through 1643 and 1644. Charles is captured and eventually confined in the Isle of Wight where he tries to bargain with various parties.

1644 Battle of Marston Moor at which Sir John Fenwick, a cousin of George Fenwick and a Royalist is killed, fighting for his King.

1645 George Fenwick is elected by the people of Morpeth to sit as their Member of Parliament in the Long Parliament.

1647 George Fenwick serves in the New Model Army, otherwise known as the Parliament Army. This differs from other armies in the same conflict in that it is intended as an army liable for service anywhere in the country, rather than being tied to a single area or garrison. As such, its soldiers become full-time professionals, rather than part-time militia. Its officers are also intended to be professional soldiers, not having seats in either the Houses of Lords or Commons and therefore not linked to any political or religious faction among the Parliamentarians. Officers are appointed and promoted on merit rather than on their status in society. Its commander-in-chief is General Fairfax and Oliver Cromwell is put in charge of the cavalry.

1648 The Royalists rise again igniting the Second Civil War, and as agreed with Charles, the Scots invade England.

In January 1649, in response to Charles's defiance of Parliament even after defeat, and his encouraging the second Civil War while in captivity, the House of Commons passes an Act of Parliament creating a court for Charles's trial. After the first Civil War, the Parliamentarians accepted the premise that the King, although wrong, had been able to justify his fight, and that he would still be entitled to limited powers as King under a new constitutional settlement. It was now felt that by provoking the second Civil War even while defeated and in captivity, Charles showed himself to be dishonourable, and responsible for unjustifiable bloodshed. The High Court of Justice, established by the Act, consisted of 135 Commissioners, but only about half of that number ever sat in judgement (all firm Parliamentarians)

1649 George Fenwick undertakes the Governorship of Berwick. He initiates the building of the Church. He is also appointed as one of the 135 Commissioners of the High Court of Justice but he is amongst those who take no active part in the proceedings.

20 January 1649, the trial of King Charles I begins on charges of high treason and "other high crimes" but Charles refuses to enter a plea, claiming that no court has jurisdiction over a monarch. 59 of the Commissioners sign Charles's death warrant and he is beheaded on 30 January 1649.

With the monarchy overthrown, a republic is declared, known as the Commonwealth of England. Power is assumed by a Council of State, which includes Lord Fairfax, then Lord General of the Parliamentary Army, and Oliver Cromwell. The Long Parliament (known by then as the Rump Parliament) which had been called by Charles I in 1640 continues to exist.

1650 The Battle of Dunbar – this was a battle of the Third English Civil War. The English Parliamentary forces under Oliver Cromwell defeat a Scottish army commanded by David Leslie which was loyal to King Charles II of England, who had been proclaimed King in Scotland on 5 February 1649.

1650 – 51 Cromwell's military campaign against the Royalist army in Scotland. After victory at the Battle of Dunbar, Cromwell captures the Scottish capital of Edinburgh and to reward Colonel George Fenwick for his contribution in battle, Cromwell gives him the Governorship of Edinburgh Castle.

1651 Cromwell tries to galvanise the Rump into setting dates for new elections, uniting the three kingdoms under one polity, and to put in place a broad-brush, tolerant national church. However, the Rump returns to debate its own bill for a new government. Cromwell is so angered by this that on 20 April 1653, supported by about forty musketeers, he clears the chamber and dissolves the Parliament by force. After the dissolution of the Rump, power passes temporarily to a council that debates what form the constitution should take. Known as the Parliament of Saints or more commonly the Nominated Assembly, it is also called the Barebone's Parliament after one of its members, Praise-God Barebone and is entirely nominated by Oliver Cromwell and the Army's Council of Officers.

Upon his death in 1658, Cromwell is briefly succeeded by his son, Richard Cromwell. Richard Cromwell is an ineffective ruler, and the Long Parliament is reinstated in 1659. The Long Parliament dissolves itself in 1660, and the first elections in twenty years lead to the election of a Convention Parliament which restores Charles I's eldest son to the monarchy as Charles II.

1706 Treaty of Union - negotiated agreement for political union of England and Scotland .

1707 Acts of Union - Treaty of Union ratified by English and Scottish parliaments.

1801 Act of Union - Kingdoms of Ireland and Great Britain united as the United Kingdom of Great Britain and Ireland.

Bibliography

County History of Northumberland

Dictionary of National Biography

Oliver Cromwell by John Buchan

History of Berwick

History of the English speaking people by Winston Churchill

Fort Saybrook by Marion Hepburn Scott

Whence the name "Saybrook?" by Harold G. Elrod

The Pequot War by Alfred Cave

Northumberland Families by Percy Hedley

History of Northumberland by John Hodgson

A British Frontier by Maureen Meikle

The Oxford book of Ballads

British Civil wars, Commonwealth and Protectorate. (www.)

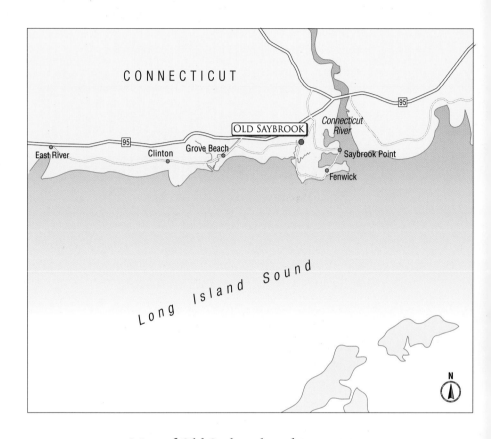

CONNECTICUT

OLD SAYBROOK

Connecticut River

95

East River

Clinton   Grove Beach

Saybrook Point

Fenwick

Long Island Sound

N

Map of Old Saybrook and its position
on the Connecticut River